To MIDGE
EXCELLENT :

JACK LICHTER   JUNE 13, 2012
THANK YOU FOR YOUR GUIDANCE

TELL ME

a Collection of Poems

Jack Lichter

the Peppertree Press

Sarasota, Florida

Book Design: Rhonda Leiberick

For information regarding permissions, write to:
the Peppertree Press, LLC
Attention: Publisher
1269 First Street, Suite 7
Sarasota, FL 34236
941-922-2662
www.peppertreepublishing.com

ISBN: 978-0-9822540-2-8
Library of Congress Control Number: 2008942136

Printed in the USA
Printed January 2009

Introduction

I once read, "Poems do not belong to the writer – poems belong to the reader." This *Tell Me* collection of poems is in that sense your property.

My choice is to write poems which carry a message. These messages are sometimes in the title, sometimes in the stanzas and sometimes hidden between the lines. No matter where these are located the challenge is for you the reader to find, accept, reject or develop your own message version. Poems are forever open to the reader. This is the reason poems are never finished.

Poetry is the art and feeling of writing. Rhyme and rhythm enhance the meanings of the thoughts and feelings, and is an aid in remembering the poem. I prefer rhyme and rhythm poems. I have included a few free verse poems needed to capture the story.

In today's world everything is rush, leaving little time for reading and writing. I appreciate that you are giving your time to read my poems. Any comments or questions you the reader may have; my e-mail address is lichter3@comcast.net. I will respond to you. Thank you for your interest in poetry and this *Tell Me* collection.

Appreciation

I gratefully acknowledge the guidance, editing and assistance of Carol Mahler, the founder of the Peace River Center for Writers in Punta Gorda, Florida, a writer's introduction and training organization open to all. In 2003, I joined PRCW and participated in writing workshops. I am forever thankful to Carol Mahler and The Peace River Center for Writers.

POEMS OF REALITY

POEMS OF ACTION

POEMS OF THE AGED

POEMS OF FAMILY

POEMS OF EXPERIENCES

POEMS
OF
REALITY

Tell Me

Best words to excite – tell me.
It is a spark of joy all agree.
Tell me – is the key to start,
opening the recipient's heart.

Children beg for this awareness.
Tell me – can be the key to openness,
a chance to amaze a child with praise,
spirit and smile become a blaze.

Seniors respond to this query,
calming their lifetime fury.
Welcome the talk and repartee,
a loving gift, better than money.

Tell me is personal recognition.
It is ignition to spur ambition.
Time spent is a special gift,
its value equal to a spiritual lift.

JACK LICHTER

Changing Times

Has life changed in our world today?
How does this compare with yesterday?
Past was the age of the big-boss mentality.
Now the baby boomers bring a new reality.

Old way employees were labor-bound.
They made the wheels go round and round.
That was the key to poor productivity.
It was the brake on employee creativity.

Baby boomers are bright and have clear sight.
They bring vision and energy and their might.
Thinking and understanding are their tools,
enough of those big-boss, closed-minded fools.

Energies grind now to speed the mind.
Efficient and faster in utilizing work time.
Thank goodness for these enlightened young.
Welcome the new way: it is much more fun.

Opponents

Athletes are the perfect study to test.
They want to be challenged by the very best.
With higher confidence than the rest,
they push themselves in the winning quest.

In business and politics, competition is key:
to succeed, it will take a better me.
Not just products and services you see,
but to show my heart, all out, full speed.

Opponent and I combine talents as one,
enhancing our skills in the contest begun.
Who knows what will be the outcome:
I won't give up till it's settled and done.

Opponents often open new directions,
leading to new and better conclusions.
Completion's value is the final decision,
lifting those who win to exhilaration.

Morality

Morality is a code of righteous conduct.
Its purpose is to control and instruct,
guiding each to what is right or wrong,
keeping us lifelong strong.

When Moses descended as God's agent,
delivering the Ten Commandments,
governments and religions chose this creed,
as God's special gift to guide man's need.

Nazism, Communism and Fascism were
immoral governments.
Street gangs of children without moral guides
face imprisonment.
A moral person makes moral choices without fear,
lives life holding family and his values dear.

Time

Time today is priority number one.
Everyone runs to be sure to get done.
Adults today seem to feed on speed.
Don't be caught in a people stampede.

Business people always push to be on a roll.
Clock, calendar, appointments exert control,
needing progress keeps them on track.
Choice does not allow anyone to slack?

Soccer moms never have a moment to spare.
Between job and home both demand care.
Drive here, drive there, must be at kids' game.
Expectations dictate be there or face blame.

Animals, birds and fish have their time-calendar.
Their clock is sunrise, sunset with time to ponder.
Migratory birds fly long distance a great feat,
flying in formation to Nature's time beat.

The universe and nature must have it right.
These do not exist under constant fright.
There measure is the seasons of each year.
Their lives not controlled by time or fear.

Would it be better, if life were at Nature's pace?
Businessmen and soccer moms with time space,
enjoying freedom for rest and to recover.
New energy and thought would be discovered.

Drugs

What is the best for me
cocaine, heroin or LSD?
These are a quick fix.
I can't face the moral ifs.

I am bold and always cold.
I don't need God I am told.
Life would be far better
without drug's deep crater.

Between high and low,
I suffering without control.
How do I ease this pain?
God, help me to be sane.

IRS 5000 Pages

Word flowed across the land,
affecting each and every man.
What freak leak news so bold?
No one would want to be told.

Speculation ran who let it out?
Was this office of the White House?
Was it the Congress or their GAO?
Was this an IRS power show?

A special prosecutor must be in charge.
Perpetrator cannot be left at large.
Effect on government and humanity
will turn the tax code into insanity.

What were the facts causing this need?
In secret I share with you this deed.
Congress in two thousand and three,
created a new tax code catastrophe.

The tax paying public was the victim.
Another government plan to skim.
5000 pages added to the tax code,
creating a mammoth taxing overload.

Meaning – more taxes had to be paid,
confusing and causing a taxpayer tirade.
Could an expert understand a 5000-page plan?
If not, what chance has mere mortal man?

(In England farcical means a short, funny stage play.)

Farcical

The best way to go is by bicycle,
unless everything is covered with icicles.
Then it is a case of staying vertical.
If not, you may land on your paradoxical.

Next best way to go is by vehicle.
It is warm, quick, and economical.
It doesn't require energy physical,
but does make problems ecological.

If by water, go by boat – that is nautical.
Remember, sometimes boats are sinkable.
Especially, when they run into big icicles.
Then they have the same problem as bicycles.

In a hurry, go by plane it's aeronautical;
do not have any problems not practical.
You may need someone paramedical,
or someone will write your biographical.

I admit this is whimsical and nonsensical,
certainly not meant to be believable.
It started when asked the meaning of farcical,
which I thought was to fart while riding a bicycle.

(NSO) National Stupidity Organization

The NSO was organized based on stupidity.
Members dedicated to be dumb and witty.
Times were tough and competition rough
Out of business didn't have the right stuff.

We were stupid, but not stupid enough.
We were gruff, our stupidity off the cuff.
New guys were organized and had no pity.
We had risen from stupidity to mediocrity?

Their guys had to be elected to Congress.
Stupidity and politics, key to their success.
Organization and money gave opportunity,
multiplying stupidity by their disunity.

NSO is like slapstick situation stupid.
Congress is pork barrel super stupid.
NSO stupidity makes one laugh, it is funny
Congress makes you cry, it is our money.

JACK LICHTER

Our leader

Strong and tall as the Eifel Tower,
man with responsibility and power
His word respected, trusted and empowering.

Meets and greets each with a smile;
placing everyone on a pedestal is his style;
learning from each makes his life worthwhile.

He listens, with no other thoughts in his head
concentrating only on what is being said.
When honoring requests, there is no dread.

Patience of a tiger hunting for food,
is his idea of fortitude,
being careful of others never to exclude.

On the other hand, my impatience is to seize control,
rapid action without thought or goal.
Sometimes my actions take a toll.

I envy his way, his abilities guide him on what to do.
His care for others is the clue.
His abilities and ways are what I will pursue.

POEMS
OF
ACTION

Relevancy

Relevancy tends to open our minds,
making new choices easy to find.
Hazy thoughts drift to hesitancy,
but clear ideas create relevancy.

Our kids' team loses a close meet.
All are enraged – it was a cheat.
Referees hold a different view.
Our team has not been screwed.

Does it take three refs to see?
Will the whole world cease to be?
Can we comfort those so stressed?
Even with the loss, are we blessed?

The time for rage has expired.
Now we must control our fire,
come to terms with this reality,
eased and justified by relevancy.

All have endured a business meeting
when thoughts off subject are crippling.
Rhapsodizing a point is a tragedy,
like a song without a melody.

Conversation too suffers interrupt,
when experiences not relevant corrupt.
How do we regain the thought?
And return to the conclusions sought?

In game or work, do not be caught
without relevancy – it is self taught.
Keep conversation on the mend.
Ask "is it relevant," again and again.

JACK LICHTER

Young Adults

Life is fun when you're number one.
All the negatives are zero and none.
Body and mind are in safe control.
One's young life is one big roll.

Does this happen in today's frantic life?
All the world brings everyone strife.
Every turn flashes, it can't be done.
Problems come by the mega ton.

It can be done, it can be done,
just not by everyone.
Let us look at what it takes.
To those that can, it gives a break.

You must have a willing spirit.
Educate one's self for profit.
Strengthen mind and body true.
Be sure God loves you too.

Nothing is easy, it never is.
Each day is always one long quiz.
Welcome all of life's tests with zest.
Know in your heart, you did your best.

Check and Recheck

There are many keys to success
Buy low, sell high is one of the best.
Check and recheck is little known
Used by the smart boys as their own.

In everyday life, check with the wife,
making good sense to minimize strife.
Another good thought, check with the boss.
Don't want to be tossed with a job loss.

Create systems to give you feedback.
If you fail, everything goes off track.
Keep in touch and observe and control.
No interruptions, stay on a roll.

When bad things become common,
you say, "How did that happen?"
Is it now too late to close the gate.
No more choice, accept your fate.

You must react before you fall.
System checks alert with a call.
Why leave yourself vulnerable?
Check and recheck keeps you operable.

Trust Is a Must

Trust is the highest level of humanity.
It's the bond insuring honesty.
With trust, we share our welfare.
Without trust, life becomes warfare.

Trust doesn't just happen – it must be built.
To work at trust keeps one free of guilt.
Parents without trust end in divorce court.
Children without trust find criminal court.

If you are not trusted, you are nothing.
You are a person, who is without learning.
Let trust in yourself be valued above all.
Let trust in fellow man be your call.

Pride

Pride is a deceiving mystery of life.
Good pride has worth; bad pride makes strife.
It is not a vision, a touch or a sound,
only a feeling which must be found.

Pride can lift you to get the job done.
Pride feelings tell when you have won.
If thing go wrong, and you lost the game,
forget those feelings and swallow the shame.

Pride can be destructive to self-worth,
in thinking we are the center of the earth.
Pride in others, like kids or teams,
give good feelings and builds self esteem

Pride can stand in your way of progress.
Any day it can impress or depress.
The key is to understand one's pride,
being sure to be enlighten and qualified.

Self-discipline

Self-discipline is the key to succeed.
All are haunted by life's maybes.
One's, first time public speaking
leaves nerves, knees and voice shaking.

Everyone has received auto driving scares,
being quick to excuse their own errors.
Self-discipline allows one to understand
to be aware of feelings of the other man.

There are times when we must subject our way.
For the greater good, we suppress our say.
It isn't easy when our experience is strong.
We know in our hearts we are not wrong.

Self-discipline means, that I cannot yell and scream.
I must stop and think what the details mean.
My goal is to control my every move,
having the strength and courage to improve.

Self-pity

Self-pity is no problem, if one is strong.
It seems to take over when one is wrong.
Self-pity is a demon of self-indulgence,
controlling one with a vengeance.

When someone close passes on,
self-pity comes like an atom bomb.
There isn't much anyone can do,
but hold tight and weather it through.

Never allow self-pity to hold you captive
break free, seize control, stay active.
There is a secret called gratitude.
Remember your gifts – change your attitude.

Election Selection

Elections are here, so we have to fear.
Political shame game makes the voters tear.
How do we know who to demote?
Which candidate should get our vote?

For us, the principle is being good citizenry.
For candidates, the principle is money.
Their only interest is being elected.
We are responsible for those selected.

Do they not know we are wise?
We despise what they advise.
They claim but never explain.
Candidates are mostly a pain.

Hearing the horrible TV chatter,
bashing candidates doesn't matter.
Make-up lies, the opponents cry,
winning is usually the ugly guy.

What are we poor voters to do?
Hold our nose and suffer through.
It is our duty to vote in these messes,
making unwillingly bad guesses.

Talking

Talking keeps others waiting.
To be interrupted is annoying.
Talk about others is gossiping.
Talk to yourself is boring.
Talk about yourself is pleasing.
Talking too long is unforgiving.
Listeners get plenty of practicing.
Silence is seldom misquoting.
Use ten percent of brain for talking.
Use whatever left for listening.

Forgiveness

Did I not see that I would fall?
Did I not know the harm to all?
What is this pain I did choose?
How do I stop this self-abuse?

Why did I not see this reality?
The answer is simple as can be.
Learn to forgive will be the key,
clearing thoughts haunting me.

Forgive myself must be first.
In this way I relieve the worst.
Next, I must confess to all.
I do not care what caused this fall.

Do it now: God may close the door.
Opportunity may be lost forevermore.
Hurry to the injured counterpart.
So they can know my change of heart.

Forgiveness brings peace to me.
I can move on and now be free.
I hope forgiveness is your activity,
so all is calm through eternity.

POEMS
OF
THE AGED

Golden Years

What could we do? What should we do?
Same as a six year old, it is all new.
Listen to commands, don't rile the pile.
Pay attention, sit straight, and don't smile.

It is like starting first grade again,
learning new habits and new pain.
Comforts of family now replaced
with senior's medicine bad taste.

Doctors replace teachers just as strict,
using big words to make one sick.
Better not to bother or tell anyone.
Pay attention to their words, then run.

The Doctor's Office

Doctor's office is the place to freeze.
Half hour waiting, my body turns to cheese.
Temperature is at least Forty degrees.
When I am called, I see his wall of pedigrees.

Cold hands and instruments chill,
readying one for the warm up bill.
You become still.
The only urge is the will to kill.

Neither chill nor bill show any hope.
Once warm, maybe I can cope.
The doctor must think I am a dope.
I insist he pre-warm his proctoscope.

Men

Young men are driven and hungry
need to have prestige and money,
usually charged with ego's fire,
filled with many imagined desires.

Many middle-age men are arrogant.
After making a few bucks, think they are gents.
Most believe they are smart and cool,
truth is many turn into cynical fools.

Old men like me have seen it all.
We know how easy it is to fall.
The goal is not to get all that we can.
It is to help our fellow man.

Thermodynamics

Thermodynamics is an engineering student's nightmare.
Difficult professors and heat-transfer formulas lead to despair.
Forty hours a week of homework brings tears and fears.
No time for students to gather, to enjoy a few beers.

My limited qualification caused me to be unnerved.
Could anything so difficult be required or deserved?
Confidence gone, my brain numbed, I was in a trance.
I could not escape – I needed this chance to advance.

Day one, I learned this teacher held us in the palm of his hand,
controlling and capturing our attention span.
Fear quickly vanished to the joy of his teaching.
I was pleased with his thermodynamic preaching.

Years later, I enrolled in a class of fearful poetry pain,
I met the teacher – it was like thermodynamics all over again.

Old Men

Useless, worthless and loneliness are ripe,
reaching out to the emptiness of life.
Having nothing to do and nothing to prove
keeps old men in a rocking chair's sad grove.

Smiles given to an old man on any day
triggers fond memories of yesterdays.
Personal identity may have melted away,
but memories are there and always stay.

Kids are gone and the grandkids raised.
Problem is, there is no one to praise.
Old men sit in nothing-to-do poverty,
a useless, worthless, loneliness reality.

Sarasota Bay

Heaven is here at Sarasota Bay
a special place, God's protégé.
It is a place for one to feel and see
into the very heart of eternity.

Sarasota bay is friendly and kind.
Relaxing and resting helps to unwind.
The dolphins fly and the pelicans sail.
Peace, happiness and goodwill prevail.

The bay breezes wash away
any unhappiness of yesterday.
It lifts the spirit; it inspires the mind.
Sarasota Bay is a gift to mankind.

loneliness

loneliness is emptiness
cold heartlessness
thoughts mindless
feelings hopeless

path to happiness
first try kindness
next thankfulness
finally cheerfulness

Sailing

Sailboats slice over the waves crest,
moving with ease and with zest.
Like seagulls flying with grace
wind lifts and propels their pace.

Unlike the bouncing power boats,
spewing odor and smoke film coats,
sailing is silent with gusts that tease,
moving only by seizing the breeze.

Capturing music from the marina,
sailboats dance on like a ballerina.
Sweeping together in harmony,
boat speed and tempo a symphony.

Sailing bestows feelings of rapture,
delivering a sense of adventure.

Eighty-One

Life is tedium at eighty-one,
moving at a crawl not a run.
Activities now no longer fun.
The only thing left is delirium.

Fools fall off life's summit.
The wise never submit or quit.
Visitors of my time are a gift,
giving me of a special lift.

No energy to keep me free.
My family has pity on me,
useless, worthless, and empty.
Is this my legacy?

Call Me, Lord

Wish to finish my life's share.
I am here and want to be there.

Work is done: sufferings begun.
Routine's a bore, no more fun.

I have known earth's tragedy.
Lord, free me from earth's gravity.

POEMS
OF
FAMILY

A Boy Knows

Sunset sky matches the heron's blue.
A boy hurries home as the birds do.
Blue skies darken the late afternoon.
He worries as he crosses the lagoon,
knowing the white water lilies hide,
the alligator's evil, treacherous eye.

He must hurry to beat the sundown,
or his mother's face will have a frown.
He knows he must make her curfew,
racing the sun as the sky loses its blue.
Breath short, he runs the last half mile.
His reward will be his mother's smile.

Parents' Suspense

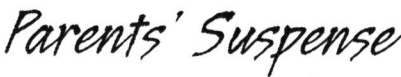

Parents nervous at son's first bike race.
They see excitement traced on his face.

Bulldozer strong, he pumps up a steep hill.
Perched on top, like an eagle eyeing a kill.

With wind in face, he releases brakes,
starting down as parents' hearts ache.

Skydiver courage for one so young,
little energy needed for the down hill run.

Quickly their son has learned biking skills.
Speed to be bird-free, enjoying new thrills.

Crowd cheers after he brakes to a stop.
Parents show fear; they are ready to drop.

Parents distraught, son smiles at being self-taught,
did this bicycle trip launch a future astronaut?

My Dad

Barrel chest man, big and strong
never to be told he was wrong,
an athlete best known to most.
In swimming and golf, he could boast.

Times were tough but he never complained.
Worked hard, pressed on, hiding his pain.
In the 1930s, all lived in grief.
Unfortunately time was not brief.

The 1940s proved no better.
War brought most all together.
Suffering took on a new form,
developing another life's storm.

For all the years and all the tears
he was there for me to clear my fears.
My dad prepared me for life's fate.
How do I begin to appreciate?

JACK LICHTER

I Married an Angel

Sunshine bright day in May
for Joan and me, it was our wedding day.
I was shaking with wedding-day fright.
Nerves tight, but my feelings were right.

Church was full with friends and family,
all truly happy, waiting merrily.
Bridesmaids and grooms stand in sequence,
holding for my bride's church entrance.

Now together for the rest of our life
my beautiful, charming wife and I.
God gave me an angel to adore:
I could not ask for anything more.

Fifty years have flown by.
For my bride and I, side by side
ours a lifetime of love rapture
with so many blessings captured.

Six children, nine grandchildren entered
to fill, bless, and be our life's center.
The kids and years have been truly great.
Thank you, God, we appreciate.

Here we are living to an old age,
cherishing all of life's stages.
Thank you, Joan, you made it be.
Please God, give me this angel for eternity.

Bridge 101

My wife is a quality bridge card player.
I am her unwilling bridge playing partner.
Twice per week I am ordered to the game,
little choice, but to smile and try to be sane.

Settings are comfortable with snacks and drinks.
Chatter is friendly; they want to know how I think.
When playing no one dares look up or talk.
I made the mistake; they gawked – I walked.

I notice players exhibit an immensity of intensity.
I struggle to stay in tune. I lack card-brain density.
My play isn't good even though I have read the book.
Make a mistake; I get a how-could-you dirty look.

Caged tigers are trained by whip to conform.
I am trained by silent glances focused as a storm.
Like the one from my teacher, I spelled cat with a k.
Bridge playing's the same – don't you dare disobey.

My choice would be to be out with the boys.
I could talk of boy toys and make lots of noise.
Except, when I get the really good cards,
winning changes my mind, it wasn't really so hard.

Bad Day

It was a sunny day in May,
bright and breezy, made for play.
It all came to a halt that night,
ending in a family fight.

What wrong caused this earthquake?
It ended for all in heartbreak.
There were no winners only losers;
shame on those deaf accusers.

How does one learn to recover
from the evil tongue discovered?
Verbal jabs make family feelings die.
How could this happened and why?

I am held in the misery of this memory,
needing to discover the will to recovery.
Will time clear minds and reveal,
allowing family to rejoin and heal?

Christmas Letters

Christmas time all sense exhilaration,
preparing for Yule-tide anticipations.
Uplifting spirits assure a happy season.
Remember, December is a time for reunion.

Children's faces mirror pleasant smiles
of expected gifts soon to be worthwhile.
All enjoy seeing pretty Christmas cards
and messages to all with happy regards.

Letters of past holiday greetings
trigger memories and warm feelings.
Welcome messages make Christmas better
received with your Christmas card letters.

Thank you for your kindness in writing.
Your Christmas letters are always exciting.

Generations

How does one compare changing times?
Decades march on in never ending rhyme.
Has the world changed each generation
without knowledge or communication?

My parents and my children years apart
never knew what was in the other's heart.
Yet each lived to the tune of their times,
presenting a different view of life lines.

My parents' time was the dark 30s and 40s.
Poverty and war were the day's drudgeries.
Clothes on the back, food on the table,
were the tasks to prove they were able.

Our grandkids lived in a different environment.
1990s and 2000s are a time of enlightenment.
Homes and schools meet children's desires.
Clothes and added luxuries easily acquired.

Kids of each time have different roles.
30s kids had shoes with holes in the soles.
90s kids wanted hundred-dollar gym shoes.
The times allow what shoes to choose.

There are differences each never knew.
My in-between generation sees both views.
We understand and welcome each perspective.
For these generations our love is protective.

Steven Gets Even

As a youngster Steven was really neat
with only one problem – great big feet.
He took a lot of teasing, ignoring that part.
He was smart with an equally big heart.

In grade school playground incident,
he step on another boy quite by accident.
Squash was the sound echoing all around,
resonating from school clear to downtown.

He excelled in high school on his own two feet
in football, track and basketball feats,
No one could move or challenge his position.
Actually, they feared his strong opposition.

Even now Steve is a runner many miles a day.
His size is awesome as he makes his way.
Little kids stand by the roadside wide eyed.
They called, "Mister can I have a ride?"

If any of you desire, a trip to the moon,
but the time and money are not opportune.
Steve can assist when his feet meet your seat.
I hope you land on your own two feet.

Lets be fair and cheer Steven's career.
Success gained with no hesitation or fear.
A word of caution for all you elite,
Steven gets even with his two big feet.

Long Term Friendships

Neighbors, cousins, sisters brothers,
friends, fellow workers and others,
with us for years on life's trip.
Make with each a deep friendship.

Our former neighbor of sixty years
now lives in another hemisphere.
Christmas letters tie us together:
our love never to be severed.

We brag of children's accomplishments.
We share grandchildren's ailments.
We reflect how they have grown.
Appreciate photos that keep us known.

At times friends or family break our hearts;
disagreements, death, divorce tears us apart.
Lost forever these long time close friends.
Friendships hurt when coming to an end.

Give your self the gift of love long term.
Stay connected show feelings to confirm.
Rewards are recorded through friendliness,
long term friendships build mutual happiness.

POEMS
OF
EXPERIENCES

Who Cares?

Is the battle of life painful?
Are every day trials just awful?
Frustration and fear the rule?
Have you bad feelings – you fool?

Has someone struck a blow
with the power of a volcano?
Did you feel the sting it brings,
proving to be a real bad thing?

What can be done – maybe run?
Seek condolences from everyone.
Will this grow and hurt as cancer,
feeling sorry may be an answer?

Is it a problem without a solution?
Is the only answer – absolution?
Is no one else concerned?
Am I alone to learn and burn?

Is there any hope of salvation?
Must there be one realization?
Is there any thought to bear?
Am I the only one who cares?

Norman Rockwell

As a boy my joy was the magazine *Saturday Evening Post*.
Each week I would rush to see the cover page.
Norman Rockwell's pictured story on the cover
of happenings touching the hearts of all.

Cover of kids shooting marbles was a favorite of mine,
connecting me to the marble games I played.
Cover of pictures of a boy in the doctor's office
waiting for a butt shot was a scary reminder.

The 30s and 40s were difficult with poverty and war.
His paintings offered local scenes equally shared.
A painting of a GI on leave to visit family for the holidays
gave a special relief to servicemen's family, friends and all.

Rockwell was called upon for portraits
    of our presidents.
These captured the burdens of our leaders
    and the why of our lives.
Paintings of Franklin D. Roosevelt, Harry S. Truman,
Dwight D. Eisenhower and John F. Kennedy
belong to us.

Time moved on, we no longer have Rockwell's paintings
to cheer and guide us along our daily pathways.
We miss his scenes of hope and life's values.
May we soon be blessed with another Norman Rockwell?

Day of Despair

A typical November day in downtown Davenport, Iowa,
the sun was shining and a perfect day was displayed.
Our mid-day custom was a noontime swim at the YMCA.
Refreshed, we entered a restaurant for a quick lunch.
This restaurant was old in a worn, downtown building.
The huge windows encouraged the sun's rays,
much like an ocean beach's feelings of relaxation.
Can you imagine the sourpuss owner half grinned,
as he was busy counting the morning receipts.
He seated us, three young hungry design engineers.
We ordered a healthy fat free lunch – no fries.
Swim and good diet prepared us for the afternoon brain drain.
Kirk, our chief engineer, now waiting for lunch to be served,
said he'd be back in five minutes after running a short errand.
Ten minutes went by, his lunch waiting, but not ours.
He entered his face grim with pain as he stood at the table.
His sunshine smile was gone, his voice hurt, his face gray.
All in the crowded restaurant became silent.
He announced, "President Kennedy has been shot to death
today.
He was in a motorcade while visiting Dallas, Texas."
My stomach tightened, my lunch distasteful, energy gone.
My mind numbed, my mouth mumbled, "How could this be?"
Bodies stiffened, tears slowly slid down everyone's face.
In the old high ceiling restaurant, the overhead fans
were the only movement, moaning in shocked pain.
Forty-one years have passed; these feelings remain the same.
November 22, 2004.

Swimming To Greatness

Swimming across the English Channel is tough,
facing waves as high as the bluff.
Unbelievable crosscurrents carry one with force.
Pull hard, kick hard – there is little recourse.

Overcoming our fear should be first,
focusing on currents and tides is the worst.
Swim crawl, breast or free style – save energy.
If we do not, someone will write our eulogy.

Twenty-two mile swim demands endurance,
a boat by our side provides necessary assurance.
Safety, direction, and feeding will keep us going.
Once started, no turning back, it is all or nothing.

Fifty-eight years ago, a youthful Florence Chadwick
astounded all with her thirteen-hour swim heroic.
The first women Channel swimmer was her fame.
She conquered the English Channel in wind and rain.

Here in the land of the Free

Is the pen mightier than the sword?
Today this is not to be.
The hand gun rules as the overlord
Here in the land of the free.

Is it no longer in God we trust?
We are the NRA victims to be.
A horrible sickness is this gun lust
Here in the land of the free.

The NRA boasts great strength.
They feed on handgun greed.
This mystery goes to any length
Here in the land of the free.

Our Presidents, great leaders, worked
for control of the hand gun need.
Could never handle this NRA quirk.
Here in the land of the free.

Pity the congressmen's morality.
When they are told what must be.
By this crazy handgun mentality.
Here in the land of the free.

A thirteen year old guns a thirteen year old.
A return injustice it was thought to be,
leaving their families in pain and cold.
Here in the land of the free.

A crowded road a fender bender - clang,
instant rage – should all flee?
Resolve the anger now – bang – bang
Here in the land of the free.

Parents are left to clean up this mess,
carrying this insanity to eternity.
It tears them apart – it gives them no rest
Here in the land of the free.

Guns denied people any fraternity.
Love of all should be our creed.
We have only illusion and tragedy
Here in the land of the free.

Can resistance and political insistence
come together to be the key
and rid us of hand gun mentality?
Here in the land of the free.

Hurricane Charley

Charley, you were a ghost-like thing.
Unlimited energy crushed everything.
High wind blast, causing roofs to detach,
roaring noise no boom box could match.
Dust and dirt swirling in the air everywhere,
leaving a path of heartache and despair.

Your land fall predicted to be farther North.
At 2 p.m., you changed your course.
Thirty minutes later caught all off guard,
damaging everyone's house and yard.
Your weapons were wind and torrential rain.
Striking fear and leaving victims in pain.

Friday the thirteenth your chosen date.
Charlotte Harbor was the open gate.
Mysterious change to a last minute path,
stirring all the locals to voice their wrath.
Homes shattered, now survival mattered.
Powerful Charley now gone and scattered.

The Incident Lesson

In the 1960s, I bought my first business.
Being young and dumb was my weakness.
As the boss, I bought a new utility tractor,
an orange machine meeting my design factors.
It could clean a job site or move snow with speed.
I expected the operators would be pleased.

The machine was delivered to a silent crew.
The operators took one look and withdrew.
A gruff fellow barked like a junk yard dog,
"That's a piece of crap," was his only dialog.
In future buying I resolved to be absolved,
seeking the expertise of everyone involved.

Forty years later, a hurricane comes to town.
Now retired, I'm asked about a building blown down.
The building is damaged, would I plan to restore?
The authorizing board told me what to explore.
Smiling pretty and knowing their apprehensions,
I sought out the managers, not the board's intentions.

I listened and learned of the managers' desires,
developing a restoration plan they inspired.
The board received the plan with distaste.
They said, "Our managers will think it is a waste."
A day later a call, "We will go with your plan.
Proceed, please proceed, as fast as you can."

Kingsway Country Club

Hurricane Charley blew in that day.
Direct in the path lay Club Kingsway.
Trees and roofs and everything gone,
can golf ever be played on?

Storm winds had left all in pain,
feelings of never playing golf again.
Leaders will rise to show the way
Charley, you do not have final say.

Have a meeting and talk it to death:
rebuilding Kingsway will be our test,
"We can't do that," is the seniors cheer
younger members say, "Nothing to fear."

Really simple their grand design,
based on the action of a determined mind.
First, bring on a golf course renovation plan,
make it sensible enough all can understand.

Next will be the clubhouse restoration,
featuring the latest code modernization.
Government is ready to give us permits.
Insurance and banks will do money credits.

When the work is completed golf play soars.
Clubhouse with elegance opens its doors.
We congratulate our leaders and their vision.
Hurricane Charley, you were only an imposition.

Golf

Golf they tell us is a blame game.
To some it has brought great fame.
To most, it is something of a ghost.
A humbling thing few get to boast.

About the time one gets feeling good.
Something takes hold, slices the woods.
If that is not bad enough, the irons hook.
Hurry back to the pro and the book.

I will have to go back to the practice tee,
to have lessons at nine and three.
Must hit at least a hundred golf balls,
or else my handicap upward crawls.

What could be wrong – is it my grip?
Can't be, did I forget to rotate my hip.
Is something wrong with my stance?
Maybe I pooped in my pants.

Pro says it is the clubs, I need a new set,
fifteen hundred bucks with no regret.
Woods will stop slicing, irons won't hook.
He must be some kind of a crook.

I will get hold; I will work it through yet.
I will hit it straight, on that you can bet.
This is the most important thing in my life.
If all else fails, I will blame my wife.

Golf Ball

Sometimes golf is a game of self blame.
Sometimes golf is a game of self fame.
Golf courses are the players' competition,
each demanding a player's concentration.

Technology made golf balls consistent.
Early egg shaped balls were inconsistent.
Now perfect in shape and weight - it's a dream.
Players are happy as a kid with ice cream.

New designs similar to NASA control,
fade right – draw left – hit high –hit low.
Weather can change the ball's flight plane.
Player can compensate for wind or rain.

Golf balls hit well is a feeling of power,
with ball speed hitting 148 miles per hour.
Ball covers are tough, centers variable design.
Concentric balls hold the putting line.

Golf is fair to players old or young
Handicap systems equate for everyone:
from age nine to ninety enjoyment the same.
Golf ball technology improved the game.

INRI

I saw his body hanging there,
nothing left not even despair.
Storm clouds turned day into night.
I was stunned beyond fright.

Life was gone from this inhumanity.
Where, oh where, was sanity?
Was this some mysterious illusion?
It hurled me into abject confusion.

I looked upon his wounded limb.
Muscle and tendon stretched thin.
Head punctured with cruel thorns,
He would have been better never born.

Ribs pierced with massive lacerations.
Face mirrored total disfiguration.
Denied the kindness of instant death,
suffering hours before final breath.

What crime could bring this misery?
What deed would merit this cruelty?
Sign above his head read – INRI
Jesus of Nazareth, King of the Jews.

Tell Me, Again

God said "Tell me."
I talked to him
And I am free.

Now I understand.
I gained spirituality
God has his plan.

My burden is gone.
Tell me was easy.
I knew who to tell.

CPSIA information can be obtained at www.ICGtesting.com
Printed in the USA
LVOW080605040512

280338LV00001B/38/P